My Fatherless Father

Pauline Osasona

Published by New Generation Publishing in 2013

Copyright © Pauline Osasona 2013

First Edition

The author asserts the moral right under the Copyright, Designs and Patents Act 1988 to be identified as the author of this work.

All Rights reserved. No part of this publication may be reproduced, stored in a retrieval system or transmitted, in any form or by any means without the prior consent of the author, nor be otherwise circulated in any form of binding or cover other than that which it is published and without a similar condition being imposed on the subsequent purchaser.

www.newgeneration-publishing.com

 New Generation **Publishing**

Acknowledgement

To my husband who supports me in every project I undertake without questions, to my children whose endearing love keeps me going in every circumstance, to my father who taught me that life is worth living no matter what situations you find yourself, just make the best out of them, to my Mum whose discipline helped mold me, to my siblings who are always there for me, and to many friends and well wishers. Thanks to all.

Dedication

This book is dedicated to my beloved father, Mr. Jonas Chukwuemeke Munonye (who should have been known as Mr. Jonas Chukwuemeka Onyeje)

CHAPTER ONE

WHO COULD THEY HAVE BEEN?

I grew up not knowing who my grandfather was, (the father of my daddy), or who my grandmother was, (my fathers' mum). It was strange. Up until now, there wasn't a single picture of them to tell me how tall, short, fat, handsome or beautiful they were. All I ever heard as I grew up was that I look like my fathers' mother, like me she was not gifted with height even though I'm not short, just average. I used to like hearing such comments, because it was the only thing that connected me with my past. That linked me with them.

As we were growing up, Daddy and Mummy would tell us bits of their past life and we would hold on to these pieces of information trying to fit them together. Trying to make sense of our existence. Daddy talked a lot about Port Harcourt in River state, Nigeria. His mum took him there, and it's where he grew up, but still it was not clear. Who were his relatives? Where are my paternal cousins? I longed to know the answers to these questions. Where were my uncles, and aunties? Where were the relatives that were supposed to make us laugh by telling us stories about how our dad behaved as a child, I guess these same questions were troubling my brothers and sisters as well. All we had were my mothers' family: five uncles, and two aunties. We loved our mothers' parents dearly. But that did not fill the vacuum. In Ibo land and Nigeria in general one is a native of his father's land, there's no inheritance from the mother's side, so something from our past was missing. There were no identifiable roots.

It was true that we had a village we thought of as ours: Akokwa in Ideato, Local Government Area of Imo State, Nigeria. But a lot was missing. Whenever we went there, other kids had their grannies and we were like, how can I explain it? We were 'tag-alongs'. We were courteously accepted. There was always a fan fare anytime we went to the village. It wasn't real. Even as a child I could feel it. Yes it was like we were strangers in our own village, and the treatment given to a special stranger was accorded to us. No roots, not at all.

THE STRANGER'S VISIT: AN EYE OPENER

I remembered an incident from when we were living in the Northern part of Nigeria, Kaduna State. Daddy had moved from Onitsha a small village in Anambra State, Nigeria where he had decided to settle down with his family after the war. He participated in the Biafran war, but afterwards he left the village for Onitsha, got a job and was doing well. Mum got a teaching appointment in a school but later left it to sell Tobacco in the new market. She did very well, she had customers and money was coming in. But Daddy decided to go to the North. There were more job offers there and he got a good one as a Sales Manager and decided to move all of us North with him. He left to start work and we were to come afterwards and join him in his one bed-room apartment. After several months he got a two-bedroom bungalow. It was a blessing, we were living comfortably. Our parents rarely let us go out because in big towns like Kaduna it was believed kidnappers were rampant and they went after children. That was between 1976 -1980. So most parents kept their children locked up inside the house when they weren't around, with strict instructions not to talk to strangers.

On one of those days, Daddy and Mummy went out and my older brother Princewell, Nkem, my younger brother Obinna, my younger sister Ndidi and I were at home when a man knocked on the door around mid afternoon. He was carrying a travelling bag. Apparently he had travelled down from somewhere. My older brother, Nkem, piped out from the window because we weren't allowed to open the doors to strangers. I came tagging up behind him and we saw a man, tall and well built, a little on the light side. Nkem asked him who he was and who he was looking for. He said he was my father's brother, from the eastern part of the country. My brother replied that our father had no brothers. The man tried to explain but to no avail. We were not convinced, we insisted that we did not know him and would not allow him in, but if he wanted he could wait outside the house until my father came back from work, then he could explain himself to him. He waited for a couple of hours, until the evening when Daddy came back and saw him. He told my father his ordeal, how we refused to allow him in because we were sure he was not our father's brother. Daddy explained to our disappointment, that he was indeed not his brother but a maternal cousin and, as we know it is the usual custom in Nigeria that relatives (even distant relatives) tend to claim brotherhood with any one related to them, or even just from the same state or tribe, for that matter. We were so full of anticipation before Daddy came back. The possibility of meeting Daddy's real brother was over whelming, but we learnt a crushing truth that day, Daddy did not have a living brother. He was the only one remaining in his family of four. His father died when he was a child. He didn't even know his father, whether he was tall, black or purple. He never had the opportunity to get to know his father before he died, his mother too was late and his only older brother Daniel died when he was small. It was devastating for us to learn all these but somehow we coped. But what Daddy did not tell us, was that he was from another village.

THE MAN I CALL DADDY

Growing up as a loner must have been very hard for my father, not knowing who his father was. But he was still able to make it in life, achieving all he achieved. It's very remarkable, but not without its troubles. Maybe that's what made him careful in life and why he sometimes bottled things. My fatherless - father. His mum brought him up but she did not live to see him blossom.

Daddy would tell us of how his mum raised him up, sending him to school when she could afford it and how, when she couldn't relatives would ask for him to come and live with them and help out in their houses in exchange for school training. One in particular did not want to send him to school, and tried to sell my father the idea that he should learn how to trade, or how to be a roadside mechanic. This made him very unhappy with that relative, so he left him and ran back to his mother. He loved school, and he would not sacrifice it. Truly my father loved education. Often he told us how he would sell all his possessions so that we could go to school, and he meant it.

It is really amazing how someone all alone was able to make it. Growing up has been an interesting journey. Daddy is someone who believes in determination, striving hard to achieve, making it against all odds. He often tells me how my determination makes him happy. He used to see me as a determined child, one that never gives up, that fights to get what she wants out of life. I think got that from him. Daddy was a great disciplinarian and wouldn't take any nonsense. I remember one day when I was just five years old, we were living in his one bed-room apartment, and he had just asked us to join him in Kaduna. At the time we were in Onitsha, Anambra State. He couldn't secure any proper accommodation before we arrived, so we had to join him in his one bed-room apartment. It was here that one day while he was at home, a visitor came to see him. I really cannot say why he did not want to see the visitor but I overheard him telling my mum that they should say he was not around. I thought it was a joke. I ran laughing to the door, raised the curtain, and shouted, 'No my daddy is inside, look at him here.' He did not find it funny at all. Afterwards the visitor left. Daddy was so furious, he wanted to spank me so I started running. He pursued me, wearing a native loin cloth in the traditional Ibo way, holding the big end with one hand and running really fast to get me. I was a very smart little girl back then. I ran as fast as my small legs could carry me. We went round the whole long blocks of houses and back to our gate. As I got there I was completely exhausted. I fell down and wet myself. He was too tired to mete out any beating, but he really scolded me. It was a day I never forgot. Another incident took place that showed how sometimes my daddy can lose his cool. He was driving us home from a school function at about 4 o'clock in the evening and Mum was expecting us. On the motor way, a driver wanted to over take him. They were playing hanky-panky on the road, and I couldn't believe it but Daddy refused to let the driver pass him. The driver swore and Daddy did not take this lightly with him; he pursued the driver, down the high way passed our side of town to another area. It was really getting late and dark before he decided to let the driver go. We spent about an hour on the road doing this rig marole with the driver. When we got home, my mum was already worrying her heart off and this was not in the days of mobile phones where you could call and find out what was wrong. She was furious with my Daddy. The food had gotten cold and as he tried to explain I overheard her telling him off, asking how he could include his family in this pursuit of a driver. Daddy did look very sheepish that day.

But the story has just begun. Daddy kept a lot of things to himself; yes he was jovial and easy-going, but looking back no one would have guessed. The following is my fathers' story in his own words:-

CHAPTER TWO

MY FATHER TELLS HIS STORY:
THE ROOTS

I had a father: late Mr Abraham O. Onyeje from the family of Onyeje Okwonagu in Abukwa Village, Umuobom, Ideato South L.G.A. of Imo State in Nigeria. My mother was Mrs Janet Nwayinado Onyeje (nee Munonye) from the family of Abraham Monunye of Umuoji kindred Umukegwu village, Akwokwa town in Ideato North LGA of Imo State in Nigeria. According to my mother, my father died when I was two years old, leaving my mother a widow and two sons, my older brother Daniel (who later passed away as well) and myself.

HIS MOTHERS' CRUEL TREATMENT

My mother's encounter with my father's older brother, my so-called uncle Orji Onyeje, was just unbelievable. As soon as my father passed away Orji confiscated all his properties, my mother's own possessions, including money saying that death had separated my father and my mother and that nothing was left for her in the village. Eventually he sent my mother away. My parents wedded in the Catholic Church which my father founded in my village Abukwa, and the church still exists today .It is where my father was a light to my village. According to my late mother, it was this church that claimed his life. As a boy of two years old I did not know if my father was black, yellow or green. My mother told me all of these stories that I am narrating now.

HOW HIS FATHER PASSED AWAY

My father was a business man at the time, a real merchant of gun powder. He did business with Government licence. He was very prominent. His associates were chiefs and people who mattered in society. Because of his business he travelled to many places. It was by associating with such prominent men that he had the idea to bring the church to his village. His gun powder business boomed. He went to famous markets in many towns in Nigeria. Because the business was demanding he had many servants attending to him.

THE DISPUTE IN THE CHURCH RESULTING TO HIS DEMISE

As founder of the church he was made head of the church committee so he was responsible for collecting and disbursing any money the church had. He made one of the committee members the treasurer. They would hold onto the money and disburse it whenever the church required it. So it happened at a time when the church needed money to carry out a project. The church authority approached my father and asked for the money required for what they wanted to do. My father in turn approached the treasurer and requested for the amount needed. To my father's surprise, the treasurer said that he never received any money to keep. When the Rev. Father in charge of the parish asked my father for the money, he told him what the treasurer said. When the money was not forthcoming, the Rev. Father called my father and the treasurer and asked both of them to swear on the bible. He told them that if they swore falsely he would give them something that would result in the death of the man who embezzled the money. They agreed and swore on the bible. Before the time he gave them could expire the treasurer died.

THE POISON

The relations of the treasurer said it was my father who killed him, they conspired together and hired a native doctor to poison my father. How did they succeeded in poisoning him? On every market day, my father would buy palm wine for his servants to thank them for their help. When they bought the wine, he asked them to share it with everybody, including himself. Unknown to my father, his enemies had gotten the consent of one of the boys to lace his wine with poison. While sharing the palm wine, the boy put the poison into the cup and gave it to my father to drink. He drank it, and passed away. The death of my father devastated my mother. She had nobody to support her; her husband's older brothers did not do anything. The person who was supposed to do something for her did not do anything; rather, he was the one persecuting her. There was no respite. Some said a woman who was married and wedded in the church should be pushed out. This was because in those days few people married in the church; it was considered an abomination. All her husband's properties as well as hers were confiscated. Nobody cared for her or her children. In the process Daniel her eldest son died.

FLEEING TO AKOKWA

When conditions became unbearable, my mother took me her remaining son, and ran to her parents in Akokwa. Before this, my mother had fought and fought to regain her husband's property, but to no avail. The matter went to court and to church authorities but nothing came out of the whole thing. She took me to her parents because she could not leave me with my uncle Orji Onyeje for obvious reasons. My mother struggled, in spite of her poor condition, to see me survive. She moved me from place to place, to her relations, although they were not my biological parents. This is how I continued to stay in Akokwa up until I grew up to school age. At this point in my life, nobody took the responsibility of paying my school fees; not the church authorities who knew how my father died, nor my so-called uncle Orji Onyeje. My uncle Orji was only interested in the properties of my biological father and nothing else. On my mother's side since I am not their biological child nobody cared for me. It was only my mother, struggling to pay my school fees. Such was my fate until I was to read standard one. Succour came in 1948, when Late Godwin, the son of Jason Munonye, the first son of Abraham Munonye, my grandfather on my mothers' side finished from secondary school and got a teaching appointment with the church Missionary Society (CMS) as they were called back then, he was transferred to Abua in River State, and I was asked to follow him, so that he would be responsible for my books and school fees. This was the agreement and I went along with him. We stayed one year at Abua town and by 1949, Godwin resigned from teaching and got another job at the Secretariats Enugu. From Enugu we moved to Port Harcourt, the capital of River State. By this time Godwin was working with Nigerian Customs. Before this time, Mr Ebenezer Munonye my mother's brother had arranged for my mother to come and stay with them in Port Harcourt. On our arrival from Enugu I opted to stay with my mother. I lived with her until I was to read standard five. Then Godwin came to plead that I come and stay with him. After much pleading I consented. In standard five I took entrance examination to Iheme Memorial College Arondizuogu Ideato North L.G.A Imo State and passed. I was the only one from our school to pass. We were told to come to the interview with £3 Pounds sterling. I was still living with Godwin, who refused to give me the money. This was in 1952... I was devastated. One funny thing Godwin did was ask me to go to the market to buy condiments for a stew, which I did because I had no options;, he could not give me the money for school, but he had money to buy food to eat. Maybe the food was more important to him. I left Godwin when I passed to read standard six and stayed with my mother. When he did not see me he came to my mother, pleading that I should come back to him. I refused to stay with him again and told him why. I told him that when I passed entrance examination to Iheme Memorial College at Arondizuogu, he refused to give me the £3 I requested for my interview. Mr Ebenezer Munonye was very angry with him for his behaviour and said if I had told him at that time he (Ebenezer) would have given me the £3 I needed. After about three months he came back again pleading that I should follow him. After much persuasion I changed my mind and stayed with him until I finished standard six in 1953. He then got married and I left him completely.

CHAPTER THREE

LIFE AFTER PRIMARY SCHOOL IN 1953

After primary school in 1953, as a fatherless child, nobody thought it worthy to sponsor me in secondary school. I resigned to my fate. The only thing I thank God for was that nobody misled me all those years I did nothing. However, respite came to me in 1956, when I got a teaching appointment with Port Harcourt Municipal Council now capital of Rivers State.

In order to qualify as a certified teacher, one had to go to teachers' college. With this in mind I took as many entrance examinations as possible and got into Ishielu County Council Teachers' college, Abakaliki in 1962. I was there from 1962-1963. One good thing God did for me, was the scholarship given to me by Port Harcourt Municipal Council, with this scholarship, I finished school in 1963 with ease. When I finished I was employed by the council, as per our agreement. So I did not go to the Labour market at all. With this achievement I was set to improve myself with further studing. Then the war broke out in 1967. I was in P.H in 1968 when P.H. fell to the hands of federal troops. We ran away to our various towns.

MARRITAL LIFE

Before this occurred I had grown up enough and

matured enough to get a wife. This was necessary since my dear mother who had been with me since I was an infant passed away in 1967 due to ill health. When looking for a wife I vowed not to take anyone from Ikwerre land where I have stayed since my youth, because I know their behaviours and what they are like. God granted me my request. I located my wife in Jos Pleatau State while on holiday from Port Harcourt. She and her parents were living in my brother in-laws' house in Jos, my niece Mrs. Isabella A. Umeh (nee Munonye)'s husband. When I saw her, however, I watched her manners. To know more about her I had to ask my niece, who told me what she knew about her. With what she said and what I observed, I concluded that she would make a good wife. There and then I started digging deep into her character to certify my inquisitiveness about who I intended to marry. When the spade work had finished, we talked . We agreed to marry. My wife is a very beautiful woman. There were many suitors coming for her hand in marriage. This was a matter of who would win her love. That time I was a very handsome young man coupled with the then "pitakwa" life. The competition was very tough but eventually I won her heart and she gave me eight children, three boys and five girls. Wealthy people came for her with their cars and other possessions, but I had nothing at all to offer. I called her and said that I have no car, no fat bank account, no houses, all I have is love for you; if you would love and marry me, you would not regret it. After some time she replied and said she would marry me. It was a dream come true.

MY WIFE'S FIRST VISIT

In 1967 she visited me; my mother was still alive then.

I took her to my mother and said that this was the lady I wished to marry. I also told Ebenezer Munonye, my uncle. My mother was very happy I could tell by her reactions towards her. A boy whose father passed away when he was an infant now ready to marry. Her high expectations however did not last long as she became ill and passed away.

When my mother was about to give up the ghost she told her brother Benson Munonye, my uncle that when she was in Port Harcourt, I introduced a lady to her whom I intended to marry, and that he should not allow me to abandon her. I was actually devastated by the death of my mother. I was left alone in this wicked world with nobody to share my problems with anymore. The only person left after the death of my father and brother had now passed away as well, so I had to plan to do the marriage rites soonest, to be married to my fiancée.

THE MARRAIGE RITES

Something happened before this time, before she ever became my fiancée. After introducing myself to Mr. Obano Okeke, her father, he asked me if I was related to one Ebenezer Munonye who lived with them in Port Harcourt before the civil war. They were under Awka Divisional Club where they would beat drums and dance. I answered in affirmation that Ebenezer was my uncle, the brother to my mum, and he said Ebenezer was a personal friend. That was what performed the magic. I won my father in-law's beautiful daughter's hand in marriage, although Akokwa my hometown was approximately twenty miles from Agukwu Nri her hometown in Anambra State. The proximity notwithstanding, who was I to win his beautiful daughters' hand in marriage especially as things stood at that time? Other suitors came to them with cars and flamboyance, while I had nothing to show for myself. It was God's work and I give God all the glory.

CHAPTER FOUR

ENLISTMENT INTO THE BIAFRAN ARMY

As a young man, during the civil war, I voluntarily enlisted into Rangers Organisation. We were trained in Port Harcourt for six months and graduated. Those of us who performed brilliantly were selected to form a training corp; something happened while we were there, training the boys. These boys we trained were subsequently drafted into the war front in 1968 when war broke out in Bonny Island and Okirka Island. Before that happened my wife and I had gotten engaged. But she did not know that I enlisted into Rangers Organisation. On one beautiful day a thought came to my mind: if the wars that had broken out in Bonny and Okirka Islands continued, eventually all of us would be drafted, and peradventure anything happened to me, my fiancée would never see me again. My family - that is, my biological father Abraham's family would be forgotten. There wouldn't be a single trace left of anybody that belonged to this family; I was the only remaining member of the family. I was worried. After much consideration, I told myself I would do something about it. The whole thing weighed in favour of my wife to be. Another thought came to mind and convinced me to leave the camp and get married; if we got married and by the grace of God, were blessed with children, people would have something to remember my parents by, whereas if I died fighting in the war the chapter of my biological father's family would close, since I am the only son of my parents left.

THE ESCAPE FROM TRAINING CAMP

Having perfected my plans, I went to the office and asked the clerk on duty to give me a pass form. I filled it out and asked for four days off, explaining that my mother had died. This made it possible for me to obtain the pass. Once it was granted, I left the camp with my bag and a pair of slippers and returned to community life. By then I was living in Mile 3 Diobu Port Harcourt. I mixed up with the community quickly and was involved with the organisation of the community winning the war effort. I was made the secretary and another person was made the chairman. In the army they say one should always use his six senses, so I used mine to go and wed my fiancée and plan our future. I did not go back to the camp until Port Harcourt fell in 1968. I left Port Harcourt with my wife and I never returned to Port Harcourt River State.

THE UNFORTUNATE INCIDENT AS A GROWING CHILD

Another thing happened in my life. After separating from my childhood friend Samuel Joshua Chinda, I had another friend whose name was Michael Ogbu, Igbo from Obodoukwu town near Akokwa town in Ideato North LGA in Imo State. It happened that on one good

Saturday morning, Michael came and asked me to escort him somewhere in Mile 2 Diobu Port Harcourt in River State. I consented and followed him to the place; inside Michael's parlour I noticed that there were benches arranged neatly. About ten minutes after we sat down the parlour was crowded with boys. I was watching curiously. My friend did not tell me the reason why he asked us to come, or what our host was celebrating. Everybody sat down on the benches as they arrived. Our chief host entered the room through a small window and brought out a big cigarette tin full of wraps of Marijuana called "Igbo" an intoxicating weed. As we sat, the tin containing weeds and a box of matches was passed round. The rule was that if anyone refused to smoke the wrap when it reached them, they would pay a fine of one shilling. I searched myself, and realised that I did not have any kobo on me and besides, what we were doing was a very bad thing. To be free from the boys and to avoid being sanctioned, I took the wrap when it came to my turn, but I made sure that I did not take it the second time. Before it came to me a second time I dashed outside and called my friend Michael Ogbu out; when he came out I told him that we should leave because it wasn't safe. Police raided places where boys smoked weeds, and if they came they would catch us and your guess is as good as mine as to what would happen to us. So on our way home I warned him that if he took me to such a place again I would not be responsible for what I would do to him. Such was how I escaped and cut off my friendship with Michael Ogbu. This all took place when I was a bachelor. I had not married yet and I was still in Port Harcourt.

LIFE AT HOME DURING THE WAR

During the war in 1968 when Port Harcourt fell, I was good with Mr Michael Nwankata, a native of Ngbai in Ideato North LGA in Imo State. We were all teaching in Port Harcourt Municipal Council. This boy was well mannered and we were very close. During the independence celebration in 1960, we stayed together in his house. In fact we were together when Port Harcourt fell to the Federal troops. After the war I had the privilege of visiting him in his home town at Ngbai

As Port Harcourt city fell, we ran to our home: Akokwa town in Ideato North LGA. There was nothing we were engaged with, until I was advised to register at Uruaka Ideato North LGA headquarters. I was appointed to teach in one of the schools. It was easy because I was teaching in a Port Harcourt Council school before the war. However, we were paid our salaries in Biafran currency during the war. This helped us take care of ourselves. Another good thing that happened to us was that I represented the World Council of churches, Anglican churches responsible for transporting Relief Materials and food to the Biafran government, their own contribution to feed the women, children and aged. The Roman Catholic World Churches (CARITAS) also sent their own quota to the government. These two world churches joined together to feed the people in the community. The arrangement was this: the Anglican Church would select their members, which was how I was selected to represent the church. The Roman Catholic Church selected their members as well. We were given Umuopia Village in Akokwa town to organise and feed the children, the women and the aged. I was in charge of the feeding centre as it was called. In fact it helped my family because we were getting all kinds of food stuff, salt, stock fish, corn meal, rice, beans, soap, cream, corn beef and more. We functioned from 1968-1969 before the war ended in 1970. This food sustained my wife and my son Nkemakonam, who he was born in1969. Another good thing that happened to us was that my niece Mrs Isabella Umeh, who lived in a house with my wife and her parents before the war, introduced my wife to the tobacco business. She got the tobacco from Isabella and would then grind it and sell it to people who snuffed. She made so much money from it. She sold snuff until the end of the war in 1970 and when we moved to Onitsha she continued to sell it until we left Ontisha for Kaduna in 1974.

SOJOURN IN ONITSHA AT THE END OF THE WAR

When the war ended in1970, our Biafran currency became useless. Only Nigerian currency was considered legal tender. Though my wife was selling snuff to people including Nigerian soldiers who camped in our town, and collecting Nigerian money, it was still not enough. We needed Nigerian money to buy food and other things. It was only at Onitsha that one could go and buy food cheaply, if one had Nigerian money. I had a suit which was made in Port Harcourt before the war while I was there. I told my wife that I would sell the suit for Nigerian money and go to Onitsha to purchase food, she agreed. I sold the suit for £40 Nigerian pounds, and had enough money to travel to Onitsha to buy food. That was how we had enough food to last us until we left for Onitsha in 1970.

The government of the then East Central State decreed that the workers, who could not go back to the states they were working in before the war, should register in the town nearest them. Before the war I worked with Port Harcourt Municipal Council in Rivers State. I couldn't go back there after the war, because the citizens were hostile to Igbos when the war ended. They blamed us for what happened to them during the war. Therefore it was impossible for me, an Igbo man, to risk my life and go back there. So I consulted with my wife on what to do. We surveyed the whole of East Central State and discovered that Onitsha County Council was the place nearest to us. Another factor that made us choose Onitsha was that the life of people at home, which we observed for about three years while at home during the war, was a bit unpleasant. So I went to Onitsha and registered with County Council Onitsha, as it was called. My first post was at Oraukwu Community School in Idemili County Council. I was there for one year, but because of the nature of the area and the fact I went to school from Onitsha town on a daily basis. I spoke to the school authorities and convinced them to post me back to one of the Council schools in Fegge town Onitsha Urban. After a year, I was transferred again to St. Michael School in the same Fegge town in Onitsha Urban. I was at this school until I left for Kaduna in 1974 for a change of environment and greener pasture.

Before this I had finished the second part of my marketing course with the Institute of Marketing Stock Port London by correspondence and obtained diploma I and 2. I was now equipped to try out another venture and a change of career. Before I left for Kaduna something happened to me. By this time I had gotten four children, two boys and two girls, Nkemakonam my first son, Nneka Pauline, my first daughter, Obinna, my second son and Ndidi my second daughter. I was living at No 9 Bishop Shonnaham Street Fegge

Onitsha. Incidentally this was the house that I discovered after the war, and I called labourers to clean it; all the doors and windows had been vandalized. It was the end of the war; there were no good houses at the time. I invited some people to come and stay with me to wait for the owner of the house. I told them I believed that the owner must one day come back. I, as the so-called landlord, used one-bed room and a parlour while others had one room each. One of us from Ojoto town had one room and a shop attached. When they offered their rent I told them to hold onto the money until we met the landlord. It was during this period that the Ojoto man who occupied the shop, which he was using as a hotel, called me one good evening and said he had seen good business. I asked him what it was. He told me that it was the exchange of counterfeit Nigerian coins. The operation was that one can take as many of the coins as possible and go to bush market to exchange them. It was similar to the incidence that happened in Port Harcourt. I told him I could not do the business; I had to tell him about my first experience in Port Harcourt before the war. You know, immediately after the war there was no money in circulation so anything passed as money. More-over I told him that I had four young children and I didn't want them to suffer in the event that I'm imprisoned as a result of such a callous act, so I couldn't do it. He became annoyed and antagonised me until I left Onitsha. I said it is better for me to be antagonised than to put myself into trouble. It was really tempting, but there was no way I could have done such a thing.

CHAPTER FIVE

◆►◄◆ MOVING TO KADUNA ◆►◄◆

When Late Mr Daniel Munonye the eldest son of my uncle Ebenezer Munonye, a brother of my mother, who was living in Kaduna after the war, came to Onitsha on a visit, he told me all about Kaduna. Daniel was staying with us in Port Harcourt before it fell to the Federal troops in 1968 when we ran back to our home town. After the end of the war, he left for Kaduna. He did not tell me the number of his house nor the area in which he was staying. So when I had the urge to go to Kaduna, I said I would go and stay with Daniel. I told my wife that I was going to look for work, that as soon as I secured a job I would ask her to come to Kaduna with the children. I had not visited there before but on the 24th December 1974, I travelled alone. I paid for my ticket and the bus left at 9 pm. Then something miraculous happened. There was a man sitting next to me. I looked at him; he resembled an Igbo man so I asked him if he was staying in Kaduna and he said yes. I told him I was going to Kaduna for the first time. I also wanted to find out if he knew Daniel Munonye who was married to a woman from Alor town in Demili LGA. He said that he knew him. I was surprised and it made me very comfortable and sure of where I was going. Both of us became friends. He would buy something and share it with me and I would do the same for him. In fact we continued like this until we reached Kaduna at 3.30 am the following day. As J. J. C. (Johnny Just Come) to Kaduna I followed him to his house at Enugu road near Panteka Market, where I slept until the following morning. I knew the place was called Charanchi Street Tudun Wada. We saw Daniel, his wife and his children; they were surprised to see me. The Good Samaritan told him how we met.

The next day I told Daniel my mission, what had actually brought me to Kaduna. I told him that I came to look for work, specifically a marketing job. So he took me to many places. We went to Zaria town in Kaduna State but nothing there was suitable. We kept on going until at last I got a marketing job with ACE METAL CONSTRUCTION as sales executive with good remuneration. After three years of hard work, I proved myself to be efficient and capable in my office and I was promoted to marketing manager running the marketing and purchasing department, senior cadre with a car attached. The managing director had confidence in me because of my hard work. There was a plan to send me overseas for a course in administration and marketing. However this did not materialize because the Managing Director A. Joledo died in 1981. However, before he died, I had been making arrangements to get employment with Alhaji Bawa Garba Electronics Company based in Kaduna. The arrangement was that I should go to East Central State to represent the company in Aba, but something happened. John Emite was sent to Aba to represent the company but unfortunately, he absconded with goods including money and a car. This man was Lebanese. I had obtained my appointment letter and I was about to go to Aba, before John Emite disappeared. Prior to this, he was told to report back to head office in Kaduna and I was to take over from him when he arrived. It was such a wonderful job, in charge of the East Central States in Aba, appointing major distributors among other things. ABG marketed TVS and Blue-Punk

Videos. They were very good products. If it had worked out, I would have been down in the East to finish my career and would have been well established there. I was in the ABG establishment for one good year as the man did not come or report and that was how I left the job.

When I left the job however I was paid my entitlements. It was part of the money I used to purchase a pickup van from the ABG Company. When I repaired the pickup, I used the same vehicle to drop my daughter off at Federal Government Girls College Bakori. This was when the college was under Kaduna state before Kastina was created and the college came under Kastina State. It was my daughter's first year in school. On my way back from dropping her off, upon reaching Jaji town I had an accident with the pickup. It somersaulted into a bush. There wasn't a scratch on my body; only the roof of the pickup was damaged. I was confused; I did not know how it happened. All I knew was that a trailer was coming in the opposite direction and before I knew what was happening I found myself and the pickup in the bush. Thank God it didn't happen on our way to school when my daughter Nneka was still in the car. Though nobody told my daughter until they came back on holiday that was when she found out. I do not know what would have happened, if she were with me. God did his marvellous work. I thank God for all the achievements I made in Kaduna while living there. I had four more children to make them eight altogether. I was able to build my own house at home. I was able to pay for my car. Even my children were enrolled in both private and public schools. My eldest daughter was able to complete her university education. Others completed their secondary education and attended polytechnics. Throughout all this we attended a church that catered to our spiritual growth.

My two daughters are married, as is one of my sons. By the grace of God the others will also get married. In all, I give God the glory for life and health.

ACTIVITIES IN PORT HARCOURT BEFORE THE WAR

While growing up in Port Harcourt before the civil war, I had the opportunity to travel to some of the towns like, Bakana, Buguma, Okirika, Degema, Ogoni, Unyada, Bonny Island, Abuka and Ahoada etc. I visited them when I was in primary school and while I was working with Port Harcourt Municipal Council, I was able to interact with the communities in Ikwerre areas. This was because I spoke their language. We would go out to watch the native dances organised by the communities and even Moon-Light Dramas. There was this native dance they organised with a kind of masquerade they called Owu. We also attended wrestling contests which was called "Egdege Wrestlers". We also went to the river to fish when the tide ebbed. We caught different kind of fish including periwinkles, lobsters, crabs mudskippers, atagbala, sungu (Ikwerre language). etc.

Though I associated and interacted with the indigenes of Ikwerre which made it easy for me to understand their dialect, I prayed to God that he should not allow me to marry anyone from Ikwerre town and God granted my request, even though I was not a proper Christian at the time. Instead, God allowed me to marry from the Igbo race for obvious reasons. As I am writing this, my God-given wife, gave birth to eight children, three boys and five girls, four of my children, men and women are married, and I have fifteen grandchildren from the married ones. I give God the glory for blessing me with fifteen grand children in my life time. God is so wonderful. He has multiplied me so miraculously that my destiny is now changed. Look at it this way; I was the only one to survive after my parents death. As fate would have it, I got married and these children have been given to me by God. That is the story of one mustard seed. To God be the glory.

MY DEAR WIFE

My wife Magdalene Nwatoka is indeed what her name represents. Nwatoka meaning 'Child is sweet'. She was everything to me when I married her. She was my comforter, when I had no one to run to. No parents, sisters nor brothers of the same biological parents. She was my mother, she was my wife, my sister and 'Obi diya' (the husband's heart). This woman stood by me despite all opposition from Patrick Okeke her older brother. She is a virtuous woman indeed (Pro 31: 10-31) She should be rewarded by God. She will eat the fruit of her labour.

CHAPTER SIX

⇥I CONTINUE: MUM⇤

This wife that the lord had blessed my father with, who of course is my mum followed Daddy whole heartedly. She would often tell us the story, of how Dad came to woo her, and that her older brother Patrick was against the marriage from the start and that he tried to discourage her from marrying him. She recalled that one day, as Daddy was coming to see her father, Patrick saw him, came charging at him, slapped him twice then sent him away. Mum said she was at the corner of the house behind the trees watching them the entire time. When she saw my dad walking away angrily, she pursued him, pleading with him not to be annoyed. Such was the love between my father and my mum. She said that her father wanted her to marry quickly seeing that she had a lot of suitors. She was fair, very light in complexion, and very beautiful. Many men with cars and money wanted to marry her, but she refused. She used to work as an attendant in a filling station, where she made some money with which she supported her older and younger brothers in school. In the school where she did her upper six, the white nuns wanted her to be a nurse but she was so afraid of blood. She loved fruits and would buy a lot of apples which her brothers kept stealing from her. Because she was so insistent on marrying my father she would not consider anybody else; her father later consented and they married. As she recalled, they were blessed with children immediately, then they moved from the village after the war to Onitsha town then to Kaduna where she had four more kids, totalling eight children. Things were good when Dad was a sales manager. He did not want my mum to work. All he wanted her to do was stay at home and look after the children and the house while he went to work as the breadwinner but this did not go down well with Mum who wanted to do something for herself. Dad was of the group of Ibo men in Nigeria who did not believe in a woman working, and he had his reasons; don't blame him. With a wife as beautiful as Mum no one will want competition. He did not like the idea of his wife calling another man sir. But it would have been better if he allowed Mum to advance herself in a career of her choice because she was quite intelligent, and perhaps the struggle they had later on in life would not have occurred. But Daddy refused. Mummy was frustrated as her children were growing up so she decided to try selling provisions in front of our house. She did not tell my father but gathered our savings and called a carpenter to install a small kiosk in front of the house. Before Daddy could come back one Friday afternoon, she had gone to the market and bought a few things to display for sale. When he came home in the evening he was surprised but there was nothing he could do about it; it was too late. Even though he didn't like the idea, all he could do was instruct my mum to make sure she closes before 8.00pm every day. This did not go down well with Mum because it was at that time that workers finished their and work came to buy provisions. Mum's genius in trading started paying off. Mummy had this wonderful way with customers. Maybe it was her smile we do not know, but she could sell anything. She did so well that she became a distributor for Coca Cola Company and other soft drink brands. They would drop off two thousand crates of minerals and sometimes she would sell everything on that same day. There were times when the demand was so much that a trailer load would be dropped off just for her.

HER RESILIENT CHARACTER

Mum has a very resilient character. She never gives up. Any time we went to the village, we would be living in other peoples' houses. We did not own any land or a house of our own. It is very perplexing to think that while we thought we were from that village. Mum was so trusting; she always believed her husband and never really questioned him. I remembered that we travelled down from Kaduna to stay with one of my father's relations, Grandpa Ebenezer. We were given a room to stay in, but when his own children arrived, we were moved and had sleep in the kitchen. Mum was terribly upset. The next day she packed all our things and we went to stay with her father in their village. The following year when we travelled, she took us to meet the village chief. He was surprised to see my mum with her entourage and she pushed us forward then fell on her knees begging for a small farmland for herself and her children, because we couldn't keep moving from one person's house to another. Was she not 'Alulu'? (A woman married into the village)? How could they treat her like this? Then she started crying. The chief was so perplexed and embarrassed that he quickly gave her a plot of land and blessed her and her children. That was how we got our land. Dad built a four bedroom bungalow and five-room boys' quarters on the land. My grandfather, my mum's dad was so full of joy that he told us not to enter the house until he came and prayed on its grounds. We waited for him to travel down to our village and perform his prayers; when he finished praying on the house, we moved in. Many people came to greet us, but I still recall that granddad said that anybody who came to the house with the intention of harming us will not survive. The following day we heard that one of the men who had gone to the house the previous day had fallen down from a palm tree and died. I can never forget it. We even found charms placed under the tree in the compound that same morning. My younger brother Obinna found them and Mum said he should just urinate on them. It is indeed a weird world. My grandfather and my father were very close and I remember that Daddy took him as his own father; he would share everything with him about his work, his life, nearly everything. Every year my father would buy bags of rice, beans, gari and tubers of yam and provisions for his father-in-law and he would travel down to the east to the village and give them to my grandparents. On one of those days when he was still riding his motor cycle he had an accident. It was very mysterious. He went home and told his father-in-law, who told him not to worry that he would take him to a herbalist to find out what was responsible. So the next day they set out very early heading for the herbalist. When they got there, my father narrated everything to him: when he was done, the herbalist asked them to wait while he consulted his oracle. As he finished his rituals and incantations, he sat down and looked at my father, he sighed and told my father that his father-in-law was the one responsible for his predicaments and that he was going to help him stop them. Upon hearing his name mentioned my grandfather was enraged: he got up and spoke angrily to the herbalist, asking how he could say that he was responsible for what was happening to him, and whether he knew who the father-in-law was? He sarcastically told him he was the father-in-law whom the herbalist was talking about, that my father was marrying his first daughter, and asked how he could be responsible when he was the one who brought him to see the herbalist and even came along with him. After calling him a fake and a liar, he took my father by the hand and asked him to come along; they both left the herbalist angrily. Daddy never forgot that incident and he even shared it with us.

My mum believed in real discipline that was unequalled and that made me and my siblings grow up with principles; even those that attempted to stray still found their ways back.

I was about seven years old when we travelled to the village for Christmas. Usually I didn't get many gifts but I was always happy and attached to whatever little presents I received. I treasured them. This particular Christmas, my mum bought a blue purse for me; it was a beautiful royal blue purse. I loved it instantly and carried it everywhere I went. I had very few coins to put inside it, but this particular Christmas it seemed as if people were not very generous with their money, and we did not receive much. Well as I was a child, I longed to put and save money in my purse just as my mum did, but there was none. Then an opportunity came; I was hoping I would get money from it. We were to visit Uncle and Aunty Ebenezer. They were old and fortunately we were not living with them anymore; we now had our own house. Aunty owned a shop in front of their house where she sold provisions and daily necessities. When we arrived we met her at the shop, after greetings, she and my mother went into the house to see Uncle Ebenezer. They left me to mind the shop. I was handling the sales very well until a thought came into my mind. I was just thinking that usually Aunty gave us gifts sometimes money, but since people were stingy that Christmas maybe I could help myself. I desperately needed some coins to put into my purse, and I thought Aunty wouldn't mind; it would be like paying me for helping her out with the shop. I took 50 kobo coins and slipped it into my purse and examined it now with money I was happy. Then I kept it. Regrettable when my aunty came back she appreciated what I had done for her, and gave me a 50 kobo note. Well that was when I was ashamed of what I had done. But the deed had been done, and quickly we were shown out of the store and we said our goodbyes. I was quiet all the way home and my heart was beating. Maybe my mum noticed but didn't say anything. We got home and had visitors coming and going and we resumed our roles as hosts. I even forgot the purse and the coins because I was engrossed in watching all the visitors and enjoying their jokes and banter. My mum called me into the room and I ran to her thinking she wanted to share something. Well it wasn't to share anything but to scold me. As I ran into the room I saw my mum holding the purse and I realised that she must have seen the coins inside it. I looked up and saw her face; it was clenched and hard. It was unpleasant. She asked me what I had done, and where I had gotten the coins from. I began by stammering that I had gotten the 50 kobo note from my aunty, and that I took the 50 kobo coins from her shop after selling some things for her. My mum asked me to repeat myself. I tried to speak coherently, but kept stammering. Then I successfully landed. My mother's face said it all; it was redder than a red pepper. She was fuming and it was not pleasant at all. She grabbed my hands and gave me the trashing of my life, when she was through, she ordered me to follow her. We marched out of the house. I was wondering where we were going, it wasn't until we made it to the road that led to my aunt's place that I realised where we were heading. I was completely embarrassed; Mum was taking me to my aunty to tell her what I had done. Oh I was humiliated to say the least. Tears were gushing down my face. Oh do not feel sorry for me, for I guess I deserved it. My, I vowed never to get myself into such a situation again. My mum marched with determined steps and we got to my grand aunt's place. She was in her store as usual and I just stood there behind my mum hiding my face from my aunt who was shocked and surprised at the same time. She looked questioningly at my mum, looking for answers and my mum shoved me forward so that my aunt could see me clearly. Seeing me crying with red eyes puzzled my aunt even more; she demanded to know what it was all about. That was when my mum began to explain to her what had happened. My aunt was not really angry but completely dumbfounded. She began pleading with my mum, telling her to just let it go, but Mum refused and demanded that I returned the coins and asked for forgiveness. I meekly returned the coins and politely knelt to beg for my grand aunts' forgiveness. She hugged me, trying to console me. It was only then that my mum's anger subsided and she consented to my aunt. She thanked her for understanding and took my hand and dragged me back home. I cannot begin to explain what that whole drama did to me. It made me think twice when trying to take anything that belonged to someone else. Mum will always be the best.

HER LOVE FOR GOD

One thing you ought to know about my mum is that she loves God. She left Catholic Church to join Daddy in the Anglican Church. When Daddy lost faith in the church we were attending because of the way they were handling the church money at harvest time, she was perplexed. Daddy would refuse to go to church; he would drop us off, go home to read newspapers, then come and pick us after church service. This continued for many months probably a year. This time may have been a time of crisis for him. Mum always asked him why he was doing this. She followed him to Anglican Church from Catholic Church and now he had left it. She would pray with us every night. Even though as children we would be sleeping, she still prayed. One of her favourite prayer then was "peace, power, plenty". Which she would repeat several times. People from all kinds of faiths were always coming to share the world of God with her, even Muslims. She listened to them and even collected their publications. I remember as a child I used to be afraid for her; I did not want her to be misled. But luckily for her she was invited to a Pentecostal church which she attended. When I came back home from boarding school, I asked after her and I was told she went to a church program. I remember that I was not happy, and I complained about how she could attend such programs? I was about fifteen years old then. She was so happy when she came back that she invited the whole family to follow her to the next program. To my surprise Daddy who has not been going to church for over a year decided to go with us, He was so happy with it that he then decided to continue with the Pentecostal church.

God had been helping Mum and Dad with taking care of us kids; I remember when we had just moved into our two-bedroom apartment and one morning Daddy was having his bath and fell down in the bathroom. Our bathroom was situated outside the main house, and Mum came running to him when she heard the fall; she opened the bathroom and pulled my dad up and rushed him to the hospital. God really helped us, they said; Daddy's temperature was zero when he arrived at the hospital, but he survived it miraculously.

Then one other day I was coming back from school. I was in primary one, and I wanted to cross the road and got hit by a taxi driver and bruised my knees in my attempt to jump off the road. It was a narrow escape. My aunty Lucy who was living with us ran and called my mum. She was at home, neighbours gathered, but it was too late the taxi driver was driving away. A Good Samaritan chased the car and caught up with him and he was asked to rush us to the hospital. At the hospital, Mum was panicking but she was assured by the doctor that I will be fine. I was taken to the theatre for an operation and stitching. The whole thing went well. I was discharged and asked to come back daily for dressing and the taxi man was tasked with taking us to the hospital every day. All that can be seen today on my knee is a scar from the accident.

Another thing that happened that really shows that God was with us, was when Mum was praying one afternoon and my younger sister Okwuchi was coming back from school with a friend; they were holding hands and working together like school buddies would do. Meanwhile Mum said that at about the time they were coming from school she felt an urge to pray, and immediately left everything and went into the room and started praying. She did not stop until she felt satisfied. As my sister and her friend wanted to cross the road a car came speeding towards them; my sister was still holding hands with her friend and she said that something pulled her back and she let go of her friend's hand. Her friend did not pull back with her but continued crossing the road and the oncoming car hit her and she fell down and passed away instantly. In fact God does answer prayers. Mum came out as she heard the noises when she saw what happened she was dumb founded. Tears of relief ran across her face and mingled with sorrow for my sister's friend.

A PILLAR TO US ALL

Mum was the pillar of our family when Daddy was passing through his job crisis. It was her provision store that sustained the entire family. Later, she decided she wanted to open a restaurant. The restaurant was very successful, until we moved house and went to live in another area. Due to the distance between the house and the restaurant, the tediousness of restaurant job and the fact that we, her children were not readily available to assist her, because we were growing up and attending tertiary institutions, she had to close down the restaurant. But by then life was not easy anymore for my mum I was in the university, so it was a struggle to meet up with the needs of the home. Daddy was aging, he did not have anything tangible to do. He later started driving commercial vehicle to make ends meet. We the kids had started growing up and becoming demanding, so commitments were mounting up for them. It was not easy. Later we were asked to quit the house because we could not pay rent. We went to rent a house in a place that was beneath us, no light, in a remote area. I remember us as children all weeping, but Mum was remarkably calm and determined to make this forsaken place a home for us. She cleared all the algae in front of the house, the grasses and rubbish places; she transformed that place and made it a little haven for us. In fact the transformation was such that the person living there before we took the house, came back, demanding to take back the place but it was too late. I really appreciated what my mother did for us. She later got a shop at the complex nearby and began selling things again, but this time it was low-key. It was really rough, life was not easy for us financially but what we enjoyed was our love for one another. Our home was filled with love thanks to Mum. No matter how little we had, we would gather in the evenings and sing, tell stories and tease each another. Such was our life.

CHAPTER SEVEN

THE HIDDEN TREASURE

Daddy continued with driving the car to support mummy's income but sometimes the car would break down and when it was working, it cost a lot of money instead of generating it. He gave it up altogether to work with my maternal uncle. By this time my elder brother Prince Nkem who achieved a very good 'O' level result, and had all A's in seven subjects he took in WAEC. He later opened a recruitment and advertising company. Later on he open a security equipment company and did very well. I soon finished school and settled in Abuja with my own family. One by one we were leaving the nest (home).

My parents moved to my maternal uncle's house which Daddy helped to build. He was given a flat of three bedrooms as a sort of reward. That was when my mum began to receive revelations of a hidden treasure. She said she would wake up in the middle of the night, the word hidden treasure on her mind, she never understood what this meant. Time and time again she had these revelations, so she decided to do something about it. She began to search the house at first, then narrowed it down to the bedroom. She searched and searched the entire house, then one day she came across a letter hidden in a book. She opened the letter and read it; this changed the whole course of her life. She couldn't believe her eyes; she was reading a letter that said my father should come home to another village and claim the lands that his father had left him. Lands;

not just one piece of land, but many. She could not believe it. As tears rolled down her eyes, she wondered how the man she loved all her life, could hide such a thing from her for thirty-two years. She did not even know that he was from another village not to mention the lands that his father had left him. Many things ran through her mind. He hadn't been completely truthful to her and that came as a shock. To imagine the poverty that she and her children had endured when he had all these lands. She remembered the struggles and wiped the tears from her eyes, folded the letter, holding it as if it were a piece of precious gold. She tucked the letter into her bra for safe keeping. She felt her body shaking with disbelief, she was trembling all over. She could not think of what to do because at that moment a lot of questions were going through her head; it was unbelievable. Could her Jonas do such a thing? How should she handle this? Who should she tell? Can she confront him with this? Where should she begin? She decided to keep quiet; she wouldn't discuss it with her husband yet. First she would discuss it with her children. They are grown up now, she wanted to hear what they had to say.

────MUM REVEALS IT ALL────

She called my elder brother first and discussed the whole matter with him. Then she called me. When she told me I was perplexed. I knew she was hurting from the whole incident. I could not believe what I was hearing. It was like reading fiction, being told that the village you had grown to know was no longer yours, and that you came from another village. It did not make sense, to have struggled in your life when you could have lived like a princess or a prince. But I recalled that one day when my father came to the university to pick me up. We were going to our local government to get papers for my scholarship, and he took me to a junction leading to a village Umuobom. He showed me the road and said one of these days he was going to take us there to show us where he was born. I was thinking that it was where he was born, where he grew up not his village, I felt he wanted to take us there, but something was holding him back. Now everything was adding up, but why he held back I could not tell. After talking to Mum on the phone, I assured her that we would continue to talk about it, when I came to see her in Kaduna, since I was going there on an official assignment the following week. I called my brother and spoke to him about it and he too was completely perplexed and could not believe it. I felt really bad for him, being a man, and what it meant to him; the village he thought was his was not; the surname he had been carrying around was not actually his real surname but his grandmother's surname. We laughed about it, and yes we made jokes of how he should think of changing his surname from what it is now to the new one, even changing his personal documents to indicate the new village. How weird, that this was really happening to us. When I visited my parents, I had the opportunity to talk to my mum about it. She called me into her room and told me about it, all over again. She showed me the letter and asked that I just listened as she read it aloud. When she finished I couldn't believe or imagine how Daddy could have successfully hidden this from his wife, let alone from his children. But I suggested to my mum that she should get my older brother over as he also lives in Kaduna, and call my Dad for a meeting so that she can speak to him about it while we were there. The meeting was fixed for the next day in the evening and my older brother came around.

GATHERING TO DISCUSS THE MATTER

That night Daddy came back home earlier than usual. After the evening meal we gathered together in Mum and Dad's room. Mum began to talk. She gave Daddy the letter to read and after he finished reading it, he was quiet for a while. On his face you could see fear, perplexity, pain and anguish. I pitied my father that day; it was as if his world had come crumbling down. That wasn't all; as he began to speak, his voice was quaky; you could hear all the pains in his voice as he spoke. I made up my mind before I heard what he had to say that whatever he was going to reveal to us was not easy for him; it must have been a terrible thing, and slowly before us he spoke. "Long time ago I have been trying to tell you all where I came from, how I wanted to take the whole family to Port Harcourt where I grew up but have not been able to do it, Yes my father ..." Then he told us all about his father and that he came from another village. His father's name was actually Abraham, not Munonye which we all bear now. Munonye was his mother's surname, he adopted it while growing up after they ran away from Omuobom his father's village to his mother's village where he was accepted by his mother's people. Wow we were stunned. One of his distant uncles had written to him a long time ago to come home, but he did not want to go back to that village. He did not even want to be buried there, and after he said that he started to cry. Oh such pain. We began to console him. I at that point spoke up that God would help him bear the pain, but that what was at stake were the lands. We thank God that all these were coming up while he was alive. We shouldn't waste time but begin to plan how to get back the lands.

His boys had grown up and they could go with him and recover the lands. My older brother spoke up, he laughed in his usual comic nothing-is-at-stake way, and said that it was not a thing to cry about, but action was needed and that what had happened had happened, and that we should begin to plan and pray on how to recover the lands. It was a troubling and deeply perplexing time for all of us. To learn that we could have been rich flowing in wealth that our grandfather had left us. It was unbelievable. Then we all agreed that the so-called uncle should be contacted and we should await his response, and if it was favourable we would then know what to do. That was how we ended the evening, and everyone departed. Daddy wrote his uncle and after a couple of weeks, the reply came and it was favourable. He requested that he urgently come back to the village, like somebody being tormented who had to hand over what they were holding. And for the first time my brother Nkem and the rest of the boys, Obinna and Emeka, began to make plans on how to visit our father's new village, or should I say real village. It was also agreed that mum should follow them whenever they travelled. They got to work on arrangements and were updating me from time to time.

BACK TO OUR FATHER'S LAND AND REPOSSESSION OF OUR LANDS

It was exciting for everybody to know that they would be going to our supposed real village. When the day they set to travel came, my older brother Nkem was driving and went to Kakuri where my parents lived to picked up everybody that was supposed to go on the journey. Obinna and Emeka were to go with them.

They set off. The journey was full of anticipation. Everybody was engrossed in their own thoughts: how will they be received? How will the place look? For my father his thoughts were: will he recognise the place again? Will they remember who he was? It was very remarkable. When they eventually got there, they got down from the car, and looked around, scrutinizing the environment. The houses, the roads, the vegetation of the land, and the people. My older brother Nkem, my Dad's first son, upon stepping foot onto the land knelt down and kissed the soil of his grandfather and his fore fathers. It meant very much to him. He held the sand of the land in his hands. The uncle that wrote the letter came to welcome them. That day the whole village came alive with activities as their arrival was noised throughout the whole village. They set to cooking and bringing all sorts of food but my parents and the boys did not eat anything presented to them. My mum began to distribute the gifts that they brought for the villagers. Oh how they loved them. They made sure that they went back to our former village, (oh this can be so confusing at times. That is the village we had grown up to know as our village, Akokwa). They spent the night there. The next day my fathers' uncle and the village elders made arrangements to show them the lands; they were unbelievable: massive plots of land. Ten in different locations. My parents and the boys were lost for words. They were dumbfounded. Tears were just running down my mum's cheeks; she let them flow unchecked as they beheld the wealth of a grandfather, father-in-law and father that was denied them. An untold peace of mind filled my mum's heart, that what had been elusive had finally been achieved. But regrets took over. Imagine being married to someone with such possessions and not knowing it. Daddy, for the first time in all his years felt overwhelming mixed feelings.

Yes what rightfully belonged to him had been restored but it could not over-rule the grief he felt over the treatment of his Mum and the way his family was treated. He looked at his father's possessions. For someone who did not know his father well, a wave of belonging enveloped him; for the very first time, he had indeed come home. This was the land of his birth, this is where he was supposed to come to at the end of the year, to visit his parents and bring his children. He was denied all these and more, and he remembered his mother; how she had suffered to keep him alive, how she would have loved to know that what rightfully belonged to her husband had been restored to her child and his children. How cruel this world can be. Life is never ever that fair. As they marched around the lands, my brothers all had their own thoughts going on in their minds: who could this grandfather be, who own such wealth and such splendour? It was unbelievable. My older brother moved carefully and slowly with his arms folded at his back; it was hard to know what he was thinking. Was he thinking of the great man he did not know or was he thinking of the lands that suddenly belonged to us? No one could tell; his gaze was fixed on the lands and from time to time he would look far ahead and shake his head. After they showed them all the lands, they promised, as was the custom to give us (our family) a land big enough to build a house among the villagers in a good location. It is call "onu obibi" in Ibo language meaning "Dwelling Place". My family fixed another date to come for that and with that they left the village to make arrangements on how to get back to Kaduna. When I was told I was really filled with joy and gratefulness to God that all of it went well. And that all our lands were restored and collected.

www.ingramcontent.com/pod-product-compliance
Lightning Source LLC
Chambersburg PA
CBHW022122090426
42743CB00008B/959